FEB 4 70

BEAUTIFUL BODY
UNIQUE BODY
LOVER
BUMMER- BOMB IN BED
MASOCHISTIC MAN WHOEVER HAD SEX WITH ME
(RTIALLY) SATISFYING
ONLY MAN I EVER TALKED

FEB 7, 70

BULLS MOVE IN HERDS.
(FROM TALK WITH KALTENBACH AT
ST. ADRIAN'S, FEB 3, 70; SEEING
MIKE STEINER TODAY.)

WHY IS MY FAVORITE FORM OF
GREETING THE RABBIT PUNCH?
BECAUSE YOU'RE ALL A BUNCHA
RABBITS.

FEB 8 70
I TELL WESTON NAEF THAT I HAVE
DESTROYED MY SUPEREGO.

SEE
HEMINGWAY'S SHORTSTORY ABOUT COWARDICE

EXPLORE → SCORE → BORE

FRAZER DOUGHERTY IS THE
ULTIMATE, A GREEZY WASP.
GREASY

FEB 9 70   ITEM ①
AFT. NEWS, WNEW-FM : A PHYSICIST
FINALLY HAD THE BALLS TO
CRITIZE PENTAGON MISSLE POLICY
AS IGNORANT (SCIENTIFICALLY), &
HE SUMMARIZED THE WHOLE U.S.
PROGRAM AS OVERKILL.
ITEM ②
        IT ALL ~~XXXXXXX~~ IMPLODES

= EXPLORE → SCORE → BORE =

FRAZER DOUGHERTY IS THE
ULTIMATE, A GREEZY WASP.
  GREASY

FEB 9/76   ITEM ①
AFT. NEWS WUEW-FM A. A PHYSICIST
FINALLY HAD THE BALLS TO
CRITIZE PENTAGON MISSLE POLICY
AS IGNORANT (SCIENTIFICALLY), &
HE SUMMARIZED THE WHOLE U.S
PROGRAM AS OVERKILL.
          ITEM ②
IT ALL IMPLODES

TO <u>HEADS</u> <u>VS</u> <u>ALKIES</u>

STARING AT LIVE BULLETS ON TABLE WONDERING WHETHER ANGUS WAS CAPABLE OF ~~SETTING THEM~~ EXPLODING THEM (FANTASY: ANGUS VISITS ME. I SPREAD LARGE SHEETS OF CORRUGATED ON FLOOR OF STUDIO & GIVE HIM EVERYTHING HE WANTS TO PLAY WITH.) THINKING OF MIKE GOLDBERG'S CLEAR ~~DESCRIPTION~~ OF BULLETS (DIALOGUE, JAN 11, 70). FOLLOWING IN CLOSE SUCSESSION

TO HEADS VS ALFIES

STARING AT LIVE BULLETS ON
TABLE WONDERING WHETHER ANGUS
WAS CAPABLE OF ███ EXPLOD-
ING THEM (FANTASY: ANGUS VISITS
ME. I SPREAD LARGE SHEETS OF
CORRUGATED ON FLOOR OF STUDIO
& GIVE HIM EVERYTHING HE WANTS
TO PLAY WITH.) THINKING OF MIKE
GOLDBERG'S CLEAR ███
OF BULLETS (DIALOGUE, JAN 11, 70)
FOLLOWING IN CLOSE SUCCESSION

ARE IDEAS:

BULLET = POWDER · LEAD

$E = Mc^2$ | E_1 → $M = E_2$

$c^2 M = E$

(c^2 = CONSTANT)

THE BIGGER THE ENERGY E_1 WHICH IS APPLIED TO THE BIGGER THE MASS, THE BIGGER THE FINAL (DESTRUCTIVE) ENERGY E_2 OR, MASS CAN BE EXCHANGED FOR ENERGY (E_3) & A SMALL MATTER (INSTEAD OF LEAD, THE SMALL MATTER USED TO

ARE IDEAS:

BULLET = POWDER + LEAD

$$E = MC^2 \qquad E^1 \leftarrow M = E^5$$
$$C^2M = E$$

(C² = CONSTANT)

THE BIGGER THE ENERGY, WHICH
IS APPLIED TO THE BIGGER THE
MASS, THE BIGGER THE FINAL
(DESTRUCTIVE) ENERGY. OR, MASS
CAN BE EXCHANGED FOR ENERGY
(E=) A SMALL MATTER (INSTEAD OF
LEAD) THE SMALL MATTER USED TO

RELEASE ATOMIC ENERGY).   5

THE WORLD IS UNDERGOING CHANGE AT A FASTER & FASTER RATE.

WHAT IS THIS CHANGE? WE MUST FOR SURVIVAL LEARN TO SWITCH OUR EMOTIONAL HIGH EVALUATION OF ~~MATTER~~ TO ENERGY. ᒥMATTERↃ

THINGS
~~MATTER~~ = BAD, DESTRUCTIVE WASTE PROBLEMS,

RELEASE ATOMIC ENERGY).
THE WORLD IS UNDERGOING
CHANGE AT A FASTER & FASTER
RATE.

WHAT IS THIS CHANGE? WE
MUST FOR SURVIVAL LEARN
TO SWITCH OUR EMOTIONAL HIST-
EVALUATION OF ~~MATTER~~ OF
ENERGY.

MATTER = BAD, DESTRUCTIVE
WASTE PROBLEMS,

AFFLUENCE, FAT, ~~MATTER~~ TIES US DOWN, PREVENTS EXPLORATION, DECAYS, CONSERVATIVE.

<u>ENERGY</u> = TIME, HEALTH, ACTS NOT THINGS, "DO" NOT "HAVE" FREEDOM, LEAN NOT FAT, MUSCULAR NOT FLABBY, REVOLUTION, EXPLORE, THINKING AS POWER, NO MORE REDUNDANT INFO.

ENERGY =

⊕ AFFLUENCE FAT
~~[struck out]~~ TIES US DOWN,
PREVENTS EXPLORATION
DECAYS, CONSERVATIVE

TIME HEALTH ACTS
NOT THINGS, "DO NOT
HAVE" FREEDOM LEAN
NOT FAT MUSCULAR
NOT FLABBY REVOLUTION
EXPLORE, THINKING AS
POWER. ★ NO MORE
REDUNDANT INFO.

SOCIETY EMOTIONALLY ~~█~~ ATTACHED TO ⁷
OBSOLETE IDEAS, INSTITUTIONS, THINGS,
PATTERNS.

TO BE <u>EMOTIONALLY</u> <u>MORE VALUABLE</u> IN FUTURE:	<u>EMOTIONALLY</u> <u>LESS VALUABLE</u>:
SOLITUDE CHILDREN (LIMIT█ NO.) ENERGY STORES IN BODY <u>MENTAL</u> █<u>PLEASURE</u>	SOCIALIZING █LARGE FAMILIES FAT PHYSICAL ACTIVITY WITHOUT MENTAL INVOLVEMENT
DIALOGUE COLLATING INFO (ENERGY)	GROUP-TALK. INFO FOR INFO'S SAKE (MATTER)

ETC.

SOLELY EMOTIONALLY ATTACHED TO
OBSOLETE IDEAS, INSTITUTIONS, THINGS,
PATTERNS.

TO BE EMOTIONALLY
MORE VALUABLE
IN FUTURE:

SOLITUDE
CHILDREN (LIMITED NO.)
ENERGY STORES IN BODY
MENTAL PLEASURE

DIALOGUE
COLLATING INFO (ENERGY) INFO FOR IMP'S SAK
(MATTER)

EMOTIONALLY
LESS VALUABLE

SOCIALIZING
LARGE FAMILIES
FAT
PHYSICAL ACTIVITY
WITHOUT MENTAL
INVOLVEMENT
GROUP-TALK

ETC.

SUPER IMPOSITION.
SUPER IMPOSING (PEOPLE).

I (t)CHING.

"THE FALSE SECURITY OF LOVE"
BOB DYLAN

"LIFE IS SECURE WITH MARYJANE"
STONES

SUPER IMPOSITION.
SUPER IMPOSING (PEOPLE).

I (e)CHING.

"THE FALSE SECURITY OF LOVE"
BOB DYLAN

"LIFE IS SECURE WITH MARYDAME"
STONES

FREUD SAID THAT THE SONS WANT TO KILL THE FATHER. HE WAS FATHER WHEN HE SAID THIS.

WE HAVE RECENTLY (VIETNAM) DISCOVERED THAT IT'S THE OTHER WAY AROUND! FATHERS WANT TO KILL/SEDUCE THEIR SONS.

FREUD = THE MIND OF THE JUDEOCHRISTIAN, GOD-THE-FATHER, GERMANJEW.

OUR FATHERS ARE LONELY _{FOR EACH OTHER.}
THEY ARE SO PROUD/COMPETITIVE
THAT THEY HAVE OUTRIVALED
THEMSELVES ~~~~ INTO
NON-COMMUNICATION WITH
EACH OTHER. THEY ARE
STUCK IN THEIR OWN AUTHOR-
ITY. (THEY TURN ~~~~ TO THEIR
SONS...) COLD WAR.

BROTHERS YOUR FATHERS [10]
HAVE BETRAYED YOU, TRICKED
YOU (WILEY JEWS THAT THEY ARE) INTO FEAR
OF THEM, PROGRAMMED YOU
FOR GUILT BEFORE YOU
WERE BORN.
EACH MAN OF THE WEST IS A
JEW & EACH HAS WITHIN HIM
THE SUCK-UP SON & THE
SHIT-DOWN FATHER.

ALL AUTHORITY FIGURES WITHOUT EXCEPTION ARE LAUGHED AT WHEN THEIR BACKS ARE TURNED TO THOSE WHO SUCK THEM OFF. BUT FATHERS GET ANGRY AT THEIR SONS.

DO NOT PERPETUATE THIS SYSTEM! DO NOT FEAR YOUR FATHERS, DO NOT TRICK YOUR SONS. KILL YOUR FEAR OF AUTHORITY, KILL THE IDEA OF AUTHORITY, MEET ALL HUMAN BEINGS AS EQUALS.

11

DO NOT PERPETUATE
HIS SYSTEM!
DO NOT FEAR YOUR
FATHERS, DO NOT TRICK
YOUR SONS.
KILL YOUR FEAR OF AUTH-
ORITY KILL THE IDEA OF
AUTHORITY MEET ALL
HUMAN BEINGS AS EQUALS

REMEMBER THAT EVERYONE REACHES ENLIGHTENMENT AT A PERSONALIZED TIME RATE.

IN THE HISTORY OF WESTERN MAN THERE PROBABLY WAS A HOSTILE SPACE/TIME WHEN THE MYTH OF GOD THE FATHER WAS INVENTED TO GIVE

REMEMBER THAT EVERYONE
REACHES ENLIGHTENMENT
AT A PERSONALIZED TIME
RATE.

IN THE HISTORY OF WESTERN
MAN THERE PROBABLY WAS
A HOSTILE SPACE/TIME WHEN
THE MYTH OF GOD THE FATHER
WAS INVENTED TO GIVE

COMFORT & SECURITY.
TODAY IT IS THE IDEA OF
AUTHORITY THAT INVENTS THE
UNNECESSARY WAR THAT
KILLS THE BEAUTIFUL YOUNG
WORLD SONS.

WHAT IS MAKING OUR CURRENT
SPACE/TIME HOSTILE IS
REDUNDANT, OBSOLETE INFO
~~xxxxxxxxxx~~ & IDEAS.

COMFORT & SECURITY.
TODAY IT IS THE IDEA OF
AUTHORITY THAT INVENTS THE
UNNECESSARY WAR THAT
KILLS THE BEAUTIFUL YOUNG
WORLDSONS.

WHAT IS MAKING OUR CURRENT
SPACE/TIME HOSTILE IS
REDUNDANT OBSOLETE INFO
& IDEAS.

DO NOT KILL YOUR SONS, DO [14]
NOT KILL YOUR FATHERS,
KILL THE IDEAS OF FEAR
OF THE FATHER, GUILT
AUTHORITY, SUPERIOR/INFER-
IOR STATUS.
YOU CANNOT SURVIVE IN
NOW/SPACE UNLESS YOU
KILL YOUR SUPEREGO.

DO NOT KILL SONS, DO
NOT KILL FATHERS
KILL THE IDEAS OF FEAR
OF THE FATHER GUILT
AUTHORITY SUPERIOR
OR STATUS.

YOU CANNOT SRUVIVE IN
NEWSPACE UNLESS YOU
KILL SUPEREGO.

MAKE SOLITUDE VALUABLE[15]
MAKE CHILDREN RARE &
PRECIOUS.

WE MUST BE MORE SELECTIVE
ABOUT WHAT MATTER WE
CREATE.

WE SUFFER FROM <u>OVERMATTER</u>.

I THINK BOTH MEN & WOMEN
ARE SLAVES IN TODAY'S

SOCIETY.
WOMEN HAVE BEEN TRICKED
INTO THINKING THAT WHELP-
ING IS THEIR ~~OWN~~ FULFILL-
MENT. NO DOUBT THIS IDEA
WAS ~~ABSOLUTELY~~ ESSENTIAL TO
SURVIVAL OF THE RACE WHEN
WORLD POPULATION WAS
LOW, BUT TODAY IT IS
DANGEROUSLY OBSOLETE

WOMEN RELEASE YOUR ~~YOUR~~ SELF
FROM THE DRAIN OF BEARING
YOUR CHILDREN, ~~[crossed out]~~ GIVE ~~[crossed out]~~ ~~[crossed out]~~
ᴧENERGY TO THE WORLD IN
MORE MODERN WAYS.

INFORMATION.
WOMEN, REFUSE TO HAVE
CHILDREN! ~~IS~~ DEVELOPE
YOUR MINDS. LEARN MORE
ABOUT THE UNIVERSE. ~~[scribbled out]~~
~~[scribbled out]~~
~~[scribbled out]~~ MEN & WOMEN
REFUSE TO ~~[scribbled out]~~
TAKE YOUR ~~[scribbled out]~~ PLACES IN THE
PECKING ORDER. IN ~~[scribbled out]~~

INFORMATION.

WOMEN REFUSE TO HAVE

CHILDREN! DEVELOPE

YOUR MINDS LEARN MORE

ABOUT THE ~~UNIVERSE~~

~~...~~ MEN & WOMEN

REFUSE TO

TAKE ~~...~~ PLACES IN THE

PECKING ORDER. IN ~~...~~

YOUR
↑<u>MINDS</u> DESTROY THE
<u>IDEA</u> OF THE PECKING
ORDER.
INVESTIGATE WITH
ENTHUSIASM WHATEVER
TURNS YOU ON.

MINDS DESTROY THE
IDEA OF THE PECKING
ORDER.

INVESTIGATE WITH
ENTHUSIASM WHATEVER
TURNS YOU ON.

FEB 11, 70

HEADLINES OF THE FUTURE:
CANCER LINKED TO
REPRESSION OF LOVE

HEART DISEASE LINKED
TO REPRESSION OF ANGER

LUCY:
THAT'S CORRECT, WE ~~WONT~~ REFUSE TO BE
PROGRAMMED BY WOMEN.
DON'T LET THE MEN PROGRAM
YOU EITHER!

STEVE: I STARTED TO LOVE YOU AGAIN ABT 11:30 PM FEB 10, 70.

I TOLD LUCY THAT I ~~UNDERSTAND~~ UNDERSTAND & LOVE YOUR WORK, WHEN SHE ASKED ME.

PUNISHMENT AS IDEA. "AN EYE FOR AN EYE A TOOTH FOR A TOOTH": IN THE MODERN

STEVE: I STARTED TO LOVE
YOU AGAIN ART II 30 PM
FEB 10.20.

I TOLD LUCY THAT I
UNDERSTAND & LOVE
WORK, WHEN SHE ASKED
ME.

...NISHMENT AS IDEA.
AN EYE FOR AN EYE A TOOTH
FOR A TOOTH IN THE MODERN

WORLD, THIS IS OBSOLETE DANGEROUS
INFO! ^ ^

WHEN MONTY REJECTS MY
SHOW FOR THE WHITNEY
DO NOT FEEL ANGER, DO
NOT FEEL AN INSTANTANEOUS
URGE TO HARM (PUNISH) HIM
IN RETALIATION, DO NOT
SEND RAGEFUL LETTERS OR
MAKE MURDEROUS PHONE

WORLD OBSOLETE DANGEROUS [21]
NEG

WHEN MONTY REJECTS MY
SHOW FOR THE WHITNEY
DO NOT FEEL ANGER, DO
NOT FEEL AN INSTANTANEOUS
URGE TO HARM (PUNISH) HIM
IN RETALIATION, DO NOT
SEND RAGEFUL LETTERS OR
MAKE MURDEROUS PHONE

CALLS.

IT IS NOT A MATTER OF SUPRESSING THESE FEEL-INGS (WHICH REMAIN IN THE BODY, PUTRIFY & BECOME CANCER, HEART DISEASE, SCHIZ ETC), THE AIM IS NOT TO HAVE THEM AT ALL. THESE FEELINGS ARE NOT INTELLI-GENT IN THE MODERN WORLD.

NEITHER IS THE TURN-THE-
OTHER-CHEEK ATTITUDE
IN THE MODEAN WORLD,
BECAUSE SADISM/RETENTION
OF PLEASURE TO SELF & OTHERS
IS A HIGHLY EFFECTIVE WEAPON
AMONG COMPETITIVE PEOPLE.
I AM GOING TO DESTROY
MY NEED FOR ANGER/HURTING

NEITHER IS THE TURN-THE-
OTHER-CHEEK ATTITUDE
IN THE MODERN WORLD
BECAUSE SADISM /[crossed out] REPUTATION
OF PLEASURE TO SELF & OTHERS
IS A HIGHLY EFFECTIVE WEAPON
AMONG COMPETITIVE PEOPLE.
I AM [illegible] GOING TO DESTROY
MY NEED FOR ANGER/HURTIN

OTHERS BECAUSE MY INTELLI-
GENCE TELLS ME THESE ARE
OBSOLETE EMOTIONS & DO NOT
~~XXXXXXXXXXX~~ FIT THE MODERN
WORLD.

I REFUSE TO PARTICIPATE
IN ~~XXXXXXXX~~ MALEVOLENT
SYSTEMS.

YOUTH DEPT.

DEPT. OF UTTER(ED) CONFUSION

ALL IDEAS MUST BE
MULTIPLIED BY t.

FEB 12 70

ART SEEMS TO BE A BETTER
INVESTMENT THESE DAYS
THAN STOCK.
SEND ART/INVESTMENT INFO
TO DALLAS (LING, JANIE LEE
GALLERY.)

I LOVE LINCOLN BUT MAYBE
IT WOULD HAVE BEEN BETTER
IF THE SOUTH HAD SECEDED.

ART SEEMS TO BE A BETTER
INVESTMENT THESE DAYS
THAN STOCK.
SEND ART/INVESTMENT INFO
TO DALLAS (LING, JANIE LEE
GALLERY)

I LOVE LINCOLN BUT MAYBE
IT WOULD HAVE BEEN BETTER
IF THE SOUTH HAD SECEDED.

UNIFORM (EDUCATION, NIXON)
PROTEAN?

THE ONLY THING THAT I FEEL
SECURITY IN IS MY OWN
INTELLIGENCE & THE INFO
I GATHER MYSELF.

GIVE PEOPLE WHAT THEY WANT!
GIVE THE PLANET EARTH WHAT
IT WANTS! (MORE CARE OF ITS
NATURE & LESS PEOPLE)

UNIFORM (EDUCATION NIXON)
PROTEAN 3

THE ONLY THING THAT I FEEL
SECURITY IN IS MY OWN
INTELLIGENCE & THE INFO
I GATHER MYSELF.

GIVE PEOPLE WHAT THEY WANT
∋ THE PLANET EARTH WHAT
IT WANTS? (MORE CARE OF ITS
NATURE & LESS PEOPLE)

MY HANDSHAKE IS OFTEN
MORE SEXUAL THAN MY KISS.
HANDSHAKES YIELD AN
<u>ENORMOUS AMT OF INFO.</u>

OUTHERE. (TO WESTON NAEF FEB 12 70)

DIAL-A-SHOULDER, SCHMUCK.
686-3061

DONT KNOW IF THIS JANETPLANET
IS ~~YR~~ YOUR REAL LOVER. ~~YR~~ YOUR EYES ARE
COOL WITH HER. ON BACKCOVER
PHOTO ~~YR~~ YOUR EYES ARE HOT,
FRONTCOVER PHOTOS AWFUL!

JANET PLAN(TAGEN)ET (PLAN-IT)²⁸
        JANET PLANET   (12THC)
                              (ENGLISH ROYALTY)
    "   ⟩PLANTAGENET   (FATHER OF)
                              (HENRY II)
    "   ⟨ PLAN-IT

SUPER(WASP)LADY CASTLE ▮ WIFE
PURE/▮ GOOD CHILD BEAUTY VIRGIN,
HOLY GRAIL TIMES. AN IRISH BOY'S
FANTASY OF THE PERFECT LADY.
VAN COPIED L. CORYELL (CORE-YELL)?
LARRY CORYELL'S WIFE WROTE
A MUCH SHORTER, FUNNIER ▮FABLE
FOR HER MAN'S ALBUM.

JANET PLAN(TAGE)N(TAGEN)ET (PLANT)
JANET PLANET
(?)PLANTAGENET (HENRY II)   {NAMES OF ENGLISH ROYALS}
PLAN-IT

SUPERNASH LADY CASTLE ■ WIFE
PURE ■ GOOD CHILD BEAUTY VIRGIN
HOLY GRAIL TIMES AN IRISH BOYS
FANTASY OF THE PERFECT LADY
VAN COPIED L. CORYELL (CORE-YELL)
LARRY CORYELL'S WIFE WROTE
A MUCH SHORTER, FUNNIER ■ FABLE
FOR HER MAN'S ALBUM.

FROM JANET PLAN-IT:

...."NOT A WAVE BUT THE SEA
    ITSELF."

[WHEN ~~ONCE~~ ALL THE WAVES ARE
TOGETHER I HOPE THEY WILL BE
THE SEA(SEE) ITSELF.]

COURTESANS..., WERE TEACHING.... HOW
TO MEASURE & LABEL (A MAN'S)(GIFTS)...& HOW TO
MATHEMATICALLY COMPUTE (THEIR VALUE).

A COURT (E) SANS LOVE.

29

FROM JANET FRAME IT:

"NOT A WAVE BUT THE SEA ITSELF."

(WHEN ALL THE WAVES ARE TOGETHER I HOPE THEY WILL BE THE SEA(≠) ITSELF)

COURTESANS... WERE TEACHING... HOW TO MEASURE NUMBER (SIGNS)... # HOW TO MATHEMATICALY COMPUTE (THEIR VALUE).

A COURT(≠) SANS LOVE.

JUICY LUCY:
IN THE ROOM THE WOMEN COME & GO
TALKING OF MICHAELANGELO,
~~YOUR~~ LOFT IS PERFECT. IF YOU ⟨BACK
LINE⟩ UP ALL ~~YR~~ YOUR ART (LIKE THE PLANETS
IN FAMOUS 2001 ALIGNED SOLAR SYSTEM
SHOT) SOMETHING MIRACULOUS MIGHT
HAPPEN. WHAT ~~WD~~ WOULD HAPPEN IF ~~ONCE~~
~~[illegible]~~ MINDS TRIED THIS
~~INSTEAD OF [illegible] RIVALING EACH OTHER~~
~~OUT OF EXISTENCE?~~ SUPER REINFORCEMENT
INSTEAD OF SUPERSHITING
ON EACH OTHER.
RIGHT, DONT LET THE WOMEN PROGRAM
YOU. DONT LET THE MEN PROGRAM
YOU EITHER.

LUCY JOINT:

IN THE ROOM THE WOMEN COME & GO
TALKING OF MICHAELANGELO.

YR LOFT IS PERFECT. IF YOU LINE
UP ALL YR ART (LIKE THE PLANETS
IN FAMOUS 2001 SOLAR SYSTEM
ALIGNED
SHOT) SOMETHING MIRACULOUS MIGHT
HAPPEN. WHAT WD HAPPEN IF GREAT
MINDS TRIED THIS
INSTEAD OF FINDING EACH OTHER

RIGHT, DON'T LET THE WOMEN PROGRAM
YOU, DON'T LET THE MEN PROGRAM

31

FOR MY FATHER:
THE ONLY KIND OF MILLINERY THAT
WILL MAKE IT IS THINKING CAPS.

ACID & MESCALINE: THINKING CAPS.

THE AGNEW SHOW IS IMPORTANT
& MEANINGFUL FOR A NUMBER
OF REASONS, BUT HASN'T ANYONE YET
NOTICED BESIDES ME THAT OFFICIAL LANGUAGE
HAS (MODERNLY) BEEN DROPPED
OUT OF THE VP'S UTTERED CONFUSION?

ALL ~~THE~~ ELECTRONS ARE EXACTLY ALIKE.
DONT BE AN ELECTRON!

NEWS ITEM LAST SUN: IN N.Y.C.[32]
THE ~~E~~ AVERAGE LENGTH OF
PHONE CALLS IN '69 WAS 20%
LONGER THAN IN '68.

I'M AMAZED AT HOW OFTEN
I SNEAK INTO MY MOLECULES.
THESE DAYS. ~~I USED TO~~
~~BE THAT~~ I'VE ALWAYS FLUNG
MYSELF AT THE HEAVENS.
HIERARCHICAL ORGANIZATION OF THE
  ATOM (NUCLEUS DICTATES TO ELECTRONS)
DEMOCRATIC ORGANIZATION OF NEUCLEUS
  (PROTONS & NEUTRONS SITTIN AT RND TABLE)

NEW ITEM: LAST ___ IN N.Y. '83
THE AVERAGE LENGTH OF
PHONE CALLS IN '63 WAS 20%
LONGER THAN IN '68.

I'M AMAZED AT HOW OFTEN
I SNEAK INTO MY MOLECULES
THESE DAYS.
I'VE ALWAYS FLUNG
MYSELF AT THE HEAVENS
HIERARCHICAL ORGANIZATION OF TH
A TOM'S NUCLEUS DICTATES TO ELECTRON
___RATIC ORGANIZATION OF MEMBER

FEB 13 70 FRI THE 13   33

(STRAIGHTEN OUT THOSE ANGLES
COMPULSIVE ONE TO WARD OFF
EVIL.)
AT MIKE ▓▓▓ THE DEALER'S
(MIKE DI GIOVANNI & ANNA)
I HAD MY FIRST S-M FANTASY
TRIP. THAT IS, THE S-M WAS
ONLY IN MY FANTASY BUT
I'VE LEARNED A HELLUVA
LOT.

34

MIKE (SAGGITARIUS) SHOOTS ARROWS.

CHILDREN'S GAMES. SEE <u>MACROSCOPE</u>, SCHÖN SCHIZ.

ANNA ██████████ (AQUARIUS) RECEIVES THE ARROWS A SLAVE TO TRAIN FOR THE GAME BUT THE SLAVE DOESNT PLAY VIGOROUSLY, IS <u>RESISTING</u>.

TOLD THESE 2 K IDEAS TO
MIKE & ANNA REMINDING
THEM THAT K IS A BULL-
SHITTER. →

AQUARIUS
MASOCHISTIC
ROBT MORRIS
JOSEPH KOSUTH
ANNA ~~MICHAEL~~

SAGGITARIUS
SADISTIC
YVONNE RAINER
CHRISTINE KOSLOF
~~MICHAEL~~ MICHAEL

THE GAME OF SURVIVAL.

I'M A GOODIE.

KALTENBACH'S CLOVEN FOOT.
KALTENBACH'S 2-WAY-GLASS
CONTAC LENSES.

AQUARIUS
MASOCHISTIC

ROBT MORRIS
JOSEPH KOSUTH
MICHAEL ...

SAGITTARIUS
SADISTIC

YVONNE RAINER
CHRISTINE KOSUCH
ANNA ...

THE GAME OF SURVIVAL.

I'M A GOODIE.

KATTENBACH'S CLOVEN FOOT
KATTENBACH'S 2-WAY-GLASS
CONTAC LENSES

36

TV IS POISON, PROTECT ~~YOUR~~ YRSELF FROM IT.

WHEN ~~██~~ PEOPLE SCRATCH THEIR HEAD/FACE/NECK, ^MAYBE TOO ~~████~~, IT MEANS THEY ARE LEARNING SOMETHING. I WATCH WHEN I TALK TO THEM.

(COMIX JARGON FOR THINKING: SILENCE, SCRATCHES HEAD.)

THE DEAD BODIES SHOW
(DUANE HANSEN ET AL) WAS
BRILLIANT.
OK HARRIS GALLERY = HOT, HIGH INFO.

FEB 13 70

~~[scribbled out]~~

I REALLY THINK KALTENBACH
IS A GOOD ARTIST.

~~WHY DOESN'T IVAN KARP
LIKE ME?~~ ~~[scribbled out]~~
~~[scribbled out]~~ (MAYBE HE DOES.)
IVAN & THE PEOPLE WHO WORK
FOR HIM (OFFICE) ARE MORE
IN(t)ARRESTIN THAN THE ARTISTS
HE SHOWS (MEEK, PARANOID, EASILY
MANIPULATABLE), FOR THE MOST PART.

37   FEB 13 16

I REALLY THINK KALTENBACH
IS A GOOD ARTIST.

WHY DOESN'T IVAN KARP
LIKE ME?

IVAN & THE PEOPLE WHO WORK
FOR HIM (OFFICE) ARE MORE INTERESTIN
IN (G) ARRESTIN THAN THE ARTISTS
HE SHOWS (MEEK, PARANOID, EASILY
MANIPULATABLE) FOR THE MOST PART

38

CONTINUE ASKING MEN: WHAT WAS THE <u>NAME</u> GIVEN TO HIS COCK WHEN HE WAS A KID.

THE NAME GIVEN TO MY CUNT BY THE 3 PROGRAMMED WOMEN WHO BROUGHT ME UP WAS: DODO. ▓▓▓▓ IT WAS LABELED ▓ "DUMB" FROM THE BEGINNING.

DAN GRAHAM SAID "NO NAME". FRAZER DOUGHERTY SAID "TALLYWHACKER."

<u>FEB 14, 70</u>

BILL KECK'S KIDS DESCRIBE

CONTINUE ASKING MEAN:WHAT
WAS THE NAME GIVEN TO HIS
COCK WHEN HE WAS A KID.

THE NAME GIVEN TO MY CUNT BY
THE 3 PROGRAMMED WOMEN WHO
BROUGHT ME UP WAS : DODO.
LABELED "DUMB" FROM THE
BEGINNING.

DAN GRAHAM SAID "NO NAME".
"FRAZER SAID "TALLYWHACKER".

FEB 14,70

BILL KECK'S KIDS DESCRIBE

39

TV COMEDIANS AS: <u>PEOPLE WHO DO THINGS WRONG.</u>
(I ASKED BILL KECK WHERE HIS KIDS GET THEIR CONCEPTION OF WHAT IS <u>RIGHT</u>).
WATCHING <u>SHANANA</u> ON/TV AT MIKE & ANNA'S EMBARRASSED ME. WATCHING ASSHOLES PERFORM ~~OPERATES~~ INSIDIOUSLY ON THE UN-CONSCIOUS: ~~TRAPPED INTO~~ WATCHING, <u>YOU</u> BECOME THE ASS. <u>MEDIA THAT HUMILIATES</u>.

S-M SOCIAL GAMES ARE CHILDREN'S GAMES,

THE TURN OF THE SCREW

PLAY MAGIC.

IF THE CHILDREN'S GAME PROVOKES ADULTS OR FEAR (OTHER CHILDREN), IT WORKS!

BUT WATCH OUT ANYWAY!
DONT HURT BACK WITHOUT LOVE.

40

ART THAT HUMILIATES: VENET'S SUPERSPECIALIZED ~~▮~~ (NONPOP) DATA MAKES PEOPLE FEEL INFERIOR ("I SHOULD UNDERSTAND THAT INFO BUT SINCE I DON'T ~~▮~~ I MUST BE STUPID")

S-M SOCIAL GAMES.

(JAKE PIERSOL) ~~▮▮▮▮▮▮~~ METHOD TO GET SUPERHIGH ON A PIECE OF HASH INSTEAD OF HIGH: IGNITE HASH WITH ALCOHOL FLAME OR BUNSENBURNER

ART THAT HUMILIATES: VENE?
SUPERSPECIALIZED ☛ (NONPOP)
DATA MAKES PEOPLE FEEL
INFERIOR (" I SHOULD UNDERSTAND
THAT INFO BUT I DON'T # I MUST
BE STUPID.")

S-M SOCIAL GAMES:

(TAKE PIERSOL.) METHOD TO
GET SUPERHIGH ON A PIECE OF HASH
INSTEAD OF HIGH: IGNITE HASH WITH
ALCOHOL FLAME OR BUNSEN BURNER?

& TAKE THE <u>WHOLE PIECE</u> IN ^{41.}
ONE DRAG.
I'VE <u>EXPERIMENTED</u> WITH THIS
<u>METHOD</u>, FOR <u>NOURISHMENT</u> NOT
DOPE. WHEN I'M VERY ACTIVE
I TAKE IN A BIG DOSE OF
CALORIES VERY <u>QUICKLY</u> (HIGH
FAT, HIGH PROTEIN, HIGH SUGAR
RICH FOOD, LOOK FOR GOOD FOOD)
THIS METHOD YIELDING SUPER
ENERGY CHARGE FOR ACTION:

STRIKING OMISSION

OF INFO, AS INFO →

42

SHOOTIN UP WITH FOOD.

UNDERSTANDING ^INTELLIGENCE OF ████ ████ ████
EATING MANNERS: EAT QUICKLY &
NEATLY. (EATING SLOWLY IS BAD
MANNERS.)

AM WORRIED THAT I REALLY
FUCKED WITH ALAN SONDHEIM'S
HEAD.

GRAVEDIGGER'S STRIKE, 33 DAYS
NOW: STIFFS AS GARBAGE.
~~██████████~~ NO INFO RE CORPSES.

SHOOTIN UP WITH FOOD.

INTELLIGENCE OF
UNDERSTANDING A
EATING MANNERS: EAT QUICKLY &
NEATLY. (EATING SLOWLY IS BAD
MANNERS)

AM WORRIED THAT I REALLY
FUCKED WITH ALAN SONDHEIM'S
HEAD.

PAULEDIGGER'S STRIKE 33 DAYS
NOW: STIFFS AS GARBAGE.
NO MEAT BE CORPSES.

43

DONT TONE DOWN YOUR ~~OWN~~ ~~WILD~~ ~~WILDEST~~ FANTASIES. GIVE IN TO THE WILDEST FANTASIES, ANALYZE THEM LATER WHEN COOLER & TAKE ACTION.

LISTENING TO CLASSICAL MUSIC AGAIN.

ANOTHER IDEA FOR <u>ARTFORUM AD</u>: A LARGE CLEAR HORIZONTAL RECTANGLE: FOR ALL WHO WANT THEIR NAME IN <u>ARTFORUM</u> WRITE IT BELOW, & THE PLACE WHERE YOU WANT TO SHOW.

THE MOST EVIL ADULT LIE IS: "DO AS I SAY NOT AS I DO."

YOU ARE ALL TURNING ME ON SO MUCH.

YOU ARE WHATEVER
YOU PUT INTO ~~YOUR~~ BODY
OR PUT ~~YOUR~~ BODY INTO.

DON'T TEACH. PLAY ~~YOUR~~ OWN SURVIVAL GAME. BE AN EXAMPLE.

I AM NOT ~~WHAT~~ YOUR MOTHER (FEEL MY ASS).

~~YOUR~~ MOTHER MAY LOVE/HATE YOU BUT SHE <u>NEEDS</u> YOU. I DONT NEED YOU, BUT I DONT MIND MAKING YOU SMARTER OR MORE BEAUTIFUL.

SINCE I CANT MAKE SOME MEN ₍SHOW THAT THEY₎ LOVE ME I WILL MAKE THEM HATE ME <u>WITH A SENSE OF HUMOR.</u>

I WANT EVERYONE TO REALIZE THAT I'M THEIR ~~GINUEA~~ GUINEA PIG.

WHAT WILL HAPPEN NOW THAT IVE MADE GRAHAM & SONDHEIM <u>HATE</u> ME? THEY HAVE MONSTROUS EGOS. WHICH WILL BE

YOUR

MOTHER MAY LOVE/HATE YOU BUT SHE NEEDS YOU.
! DONT NEED YOU, BUT I DONT

AFFECTED HOW? 46
ALAN SONDHEIM THINKS HE'S
GOD. THIS IS EVIL.
HOW HE'LL RESPOND TO MY INFO
WILL BE AN IMPORTANT TEST.

I WANT EVERYONE TO REALIZE
THAT I'M THEIR ~~GINUEA~~
~~████████ ████~~. GUINEA PIG.
I'M ~~YOUR GUINEA████████~~ PIG.
WATCH WHAT HAPPENS TO ME.

MOTHERFUCKER
MA'FUGGER
MA'FUGGA
MOTHERFATHER

NOT <u>WATCH ME</u>, ^BUT: FIND OUT WHAT 47
<u>HAPPENS TO ME</u>^.

WEEDS DYING? TRY <u>GROWING</u>
<u>TESQUE</u>.

<u>I **WANT**</u> <u>EVERYBODY</u> TO BE <u>GREAT</u>.
"   "   TO LOVE <u>ALL MATTER</u>.
                        ALMA ■MATER
                        ALL MY MATERS MATTERS
                        ALL MY MOTHERFATHERS.
"   "   <u>BRAINS TO WORK</u>
          →<u>HARDER, BE BIGGER</u>,

USE MORE OF THEMSELVES,[48]
WAKE UP.
JOY FROM THE MIND.

THE MIND IS A MUSCLE.
(YUONNE RAINER).
EXERCISE IT! THINK
INVENTIVELY.

POOL OUR MIND POWER.

KILL THE WITCH GAMES (NOT THE WITCHES).
USE WITCH INFO TO BENEFIT WORLD.

TRANSCONTINENTAL IDEAS HOOKUP. WORLD HEADS UNITE ~~OR~~ YOUR BRAIN POWER, SHARE IT WITH WHOLE WORLD

NO SECRETS!

→ WATCH OUT FOR THE
(L?)<u>OVERS</u>.

→ <u>OVERLOVE MAY</u>
<u>KILL</u> <u>ALSO</u>.

WORLD MINDS,
INVESTIGATE LOVE.

WORLD HEADS UNITE!
PROJECT OUR POWER
INTO THE UNIVERSE!
TRANSMIT ISOMETRICALLY.
CAUTION: WHAT DO WE TRANSMIT?
LOVE? WILL WORLD LOVE
TRANSMIT OVER —
EXCITE?

MAIN IDEA:
SAVE THE WORLD BRAIN

I WANNA LOVE.
I WANNA CONSORT.
I WANNA LOVE & WORK WITH
A <u>GREAT MAN</u>, WHOSE
IDEAS HAPPEN TO GO
ALONG THE SAME LINES
→AS MINE, & WHOSE & MY
DIFFERENCES (HAVING TROUBLE
WITH THE DIFFERENCES, LOZANO?)

NO

SEE P. 53

STIMULATE EACH OTHER.⁵²

ARTFORUM AD (ANOTHER NEW ONE):

LEE LOZANO
WAVES
AT THE
WHITNEY.
WHITNEY MUSEUM, NOV ---, 70 (ETC)

WHAT I'D REALLY LIKE TO TRY
IS HAVING THE SHOW ON GOLD
WALLS (~~DARK~~ BETTER THAN BLACK?)

SEE PHOTOS PHYSICS TODAY
FEB 70 PP 34-5

WHAT I'D REALLY LIKE TO TRY IS SOMETHING LIKE SHOWING WAVES ON WALLS COMPLETELY COVERED WITH PHOTOS OF THE HEAVENS.

HOW ABT NEGATIVE SHOTS OF STARS, THAT IS (NO PUNS) DARK STARS ON LIGHT GRAY SPACE. (OVER)

WHAT I'D REALLY LIKE
TO TRY IS SOMETHING
LIKE SHOWING WAVES
ON WALLS COMPLETELY
COVERED WITH PHOTOS
OF THE HEAVENS.

HOW ABT NEGATIVE
SHOTS OF STARS THAT IS
(NO FUNS) DARK STARS
GRAY SPACE. (OVER)

WANT TO ASSOCIATE
PAINTING WITH PLEASURE
AGAIN: A MOVING EXPERI-
ENCE FOR ALL ARTISTS
& ~~XXXXXXXXXX~~ YIPPIES & HEADS
& TOURISTS & ANYONE.
MAKE PAINTING:
AN EXCITING TRIP, A FEW
MOMENTS PEOPLE WILL RE-
MEMBER.

INFORMAL ~~XXXX~~ CLOTHES ⟶

FOR MY OPENING AT THE WHITNEY I WOULD LIKE TO DO A VERY SPECIAL FANCY:

WANT TO GIVE AN INVITATION PERSONALLY TO THE DOWNTOWN PEOPLE I KNOW FROM BEING/LIVING IN THIS NEIGHBORHOOD FOR SO LONG. IN FACT THESE ARE THE ONLY PEOPLE I WANT AT MY OPENING. JUST NEIGHBORHOOD PEOPLE: FROM DRUGSTORES, FOOD & LAUNDRY STORES ETC. GET IT? (OVER)

STATIONERY STORES

IDEAS ARE THE MOST
POWERFUL THING IN
THE WORLD.

PISS? WATCH OUT.
PASS ON IDEAS.
(NEVER MIND WHO GETS
THE CREDIT FOR THEM,
YOU RIVAL RABBITS.)
GIVE AWAY YOUR IDEAS.

ALSO ALL THE PEOPLE IN
THE BUILDING, MIKE & ANNA
ED & CINDY & OTHERS, ~~LANDLORD~~ STEVE & ANN KELSEY
~~LAWYER~~ JERRY ORDOVER ~~CROCCO~~ LOU SGROI

A DISPLACEMENT THAT
INTERESTS ME. STIMULATE
THEIR MINDS WITH NEW EX-
PERIENCE, HOPE THEY HAVE
DIALOGUE WITH EACH OTHER.
MEET YOUR ~~THE~~ ENVIRONMENT.

ALSO ALL THE PEOPLE IN
THE BUILDING, MIKE & ANNA
ED & CINDY & OTHERS
ON SG801

A DISPLACEMENT THAT
INTERESTS ME. STIMULATE
THEIR MINDS WITH NEW EX-
PERIENCE, HOPE THEY HAVE
DIALOGUE WITH EACH OTHER
MEET XX ENVIRONMENT

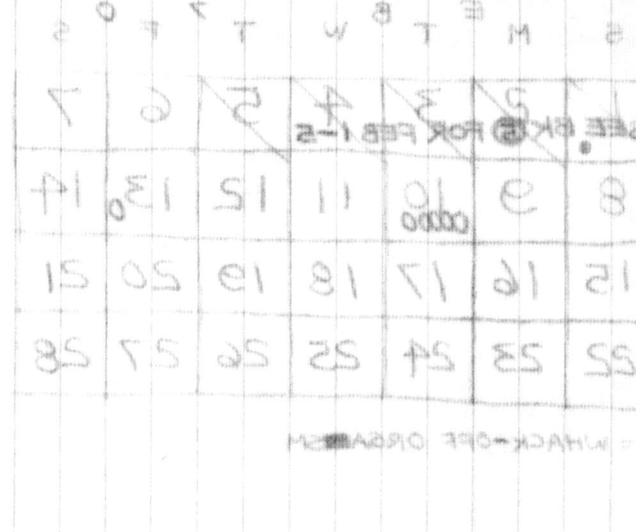

S	M	T	W	T	F	S
1 SEE BK (5) FOR FEB 1-5	2	3	4	5	6	7
8	9	10 ooooo	11	12	13 o	14
15	16	17	18	19	20	21
22	23	24	25	26	27	28

0 = WHACK-OFF ORGASM

Lee Lozano
Private Book 6

1970
Edited January 27, 1972

Publication © 2019
The Estate of Lee Lozano
and Karma Books, New York

Courtesy Hauser & Wirth

ISBN 978-1-949172-10-2